ON
YOUR
MARK

Devotionals for families with young children by William L. Coleman

---

Counting Stars, meditations on God's creation.

My Magnificent Machine, devotionals centered around the marvels of the human body.

Listen to the Animals, lessons from the animal world.

On Your Mark, challenges from the lives of well-known athletes.

The Good Night Book, bedtime inspirationals (especially for those who may be afraid of the dark).

ON YOUR MARK

William L. Coleman

Bethany Fellowship INC.
MINNEAPOLIS,
MINNESOTA 55438

Design: Koechel/Peterson Design, Minneapolis, Mn.

Photo credits: Pp. 22, 30, 39, 40, 59, 71, 78, 80, 91, 99, 101, 104, and 109,
    Wide World Photos.
    Pp. 8, 16, 48, 53, 92, The Minneapolis Star.
    Pp. 12 and 68, The Minnesota Vikings.
All other photos by Koechel/Peterson Design, Minneapolis, Mn.

Verses marked TLB are taken from The Living Bible, copyright 1971 by
Tyndale House Publishers, Wheaton, Ill. Used by permission.

Copyright © 1979
William L. Coleman
All rights reserved

Published by Bethany Fellowship, Inc.
6820 Auto Club Road, Minneapolis, Minnesota 55438

Printed in the United States of America

Library of Congress Cataloging in Publication Data

Coleman, William L.
    On your mark.

    SUMMARY: Presents outstanding events and people from the world
of sports, adding inspirational questions and messages at the end of each
selection.
    1. Family—Prayer-books and devotions—English. 2. Sports.
[1. Prayer books and devotions. 2. Sports]
I. Title.
BV255.C734   242   79-16458
ISBN 0-87123-490-4

Contents

Acknowledgement

Special thanks to Jim Coleman for reading and helping to complete the manuscript.

Biographical Sketch

WILLIAM L. COLEMAN is a graduate of the Washington Bible College in Washington, D.C., and Grace Theological Seminary in Winona Lake, Indiana.

He has pastored three churches: a Baptist church in Michigan, a Mennonite church in Kansas and an Evangelical Free Church in Aurora, Nebraska. He is a Staley Foundation lecturer.

The author of 75 magazine articles, his by-line has appeared in *Christianity Today, Eternity, Good News Broadcaster, Campus Life, Moody Monthly, Evangelical Beacon,* and *The Christian Reader.* This is Coleman's fourth children's book.

Enjoying Sports

Whether young or old, most of us like sports. They are fun to play and exciting to watch. This is a collection of spectacular sports events and characters. I think you will spend several enjoyable hours reading these amazing accomplishments.

Sports are like life. Both are packed with stories of courage, dedication, sacrifice, victory and defeat. In this book we try to apply some of these illustrations to our daily lives. A few of the athletes are Christians—most are not. Yet what they have done can teach us to guide our lives.

Read these stories and enjoy them. As you read you might find yourself growing just a little more.

William L. Coleman
Aurora, Nebraska

Roger Staubach, quarterback of the Dallas Cowboys, eludes the fearsome Minnesota Viking front four.

Diane
310-92-3296

one

Nearly Perfect

Looking for a fantastic athlete? Check out quarterback Roger Staubach. He has starred in several sports, so the National Football League was fortunate he chose to play their sport.

Staubach entered the Naval Academy at Annapolis to become a career officer. In his spare time he worked out and participated in a number of sports. While there he collected seven letters for basketball, football and baseball.

Before his four years were over he would become one of the best athletes to ever attend the Academy.

Part of Staubach's success came from his natural talent. Athletics came easy to him. But this didn't mean he didn't work hard. Staubach trained so much that doctors discovered he had less fat in his body than any other player in the National Football League.

When Roger graduated from college he had won the Camp Memorial Trophy, the Maxwell Trophy, and the Athletic Association Award. He also won the Thompson Award for the third time as best athlete at the Academy.

In his junior year he won the Heisman Trophy. Only a handful of players have won it that early in college. Roger was named the best college football player in the nation. The Academy decided to retire his number (12) so no one else would wear it.

What does a man do with all of these honors? Normally he would become a professional football player. Roger was just what they were looking for. He weighed about 200 pounds and stood 6 foot 3 inches.

They wanted Staubach in professional football but the Navy also wanted him. He had agreed to serve for almost four years after graduation and he intended to keep his promise.

The Dallas Cowboys were so impressed they selected Staubach anyway. They were willing to wait four years for this athlete. During those years the Cowboys paid Roger $500 a month while he was in the Navy. They also paid him a large amount for signing.

It was a huge gamble to take. No one had ever stayed out of football for four years and then made it as a star. During this time Staubach spent one year in the Viet Nam war. Could he come back and play?

In 1969 the Dallas Cowboys had a chance to answer the question. Roger Staubach finished his Navy duty and reported to professional football.

Two years later he became the starting quarterback. Staubach threw for 1,900 yards. He completed almost 60% of his passes. Everyone knew Roger could star in the NFL.

By 1979 Roger had led the Cowboys to five Super Bowls. They had played Denver, Miami, Baltimore and Pittsburgh twice. The Cowboys had become one of the strongest teams in football. Their main quarterback was a color-blind sailor who was in great shape.

If Roger is an outstanding quarterback, he is still only nearly perfect. He has had bad days and does some things he isn't proud of. But is it his personal faith that helps make up the man? He said it this way: "I feel very fortunate to have a personal relationship with Christ."

It would be too bad if we did so many good things in life and missed the most important. Jesus Christ would like to live at the center of your life.

"Let not your heart be troubled. You are trusting God, now trust in me" (John 14:1, TLB).

1. Name two awards Staubach won in college.
2. What happened to Staubach's college number?

I need to invite Jesus Christ to live inside me.

Minnesota Viking defensive end Jim Marshall puts pressure on the Detroit Lions' quarterback.

two

The Wrong Way

There aren't many players who get into the Football Hall of Fame while their career is still going. Jim Marshall got there early, and sometimes he wishes he hadn't.

Marshall has one of the hardest jobs in football. He is a defensive lineman. When the other team has the ball, he goes in the game and tries to stop them.

Maybe a fast runner like O. J. Simpson will come running like a wild horse. Marshall's job is to hit him low and hard. If at all possible he has to keep the "Juice" from gaining any ground.

But sometimes the quarterback will keep the ball and drop back to pass. Then the defensive lineman has to hurry past the opposing players and try to tackle him before he can throw it.

Usually defensive linemen are big and fast—maybe 6 feet 4 inches and 260 pounds. Bob Lilly of Dallas was one of the most famous. In 1964 there wasn't a single play in which one man could stop Lilly. Often two men couldn't hold him out, and sometimes three weren't enough.

These men don't have to remember a lot of plays. When the ball is hiked, their job is simple: Go after the man with the pigskin.

Bubba Smith was one of the most famous linemen. He played for Baltimore and Oakland. Bubba was 6 feet 7 inches tall and weighed 300 pounds.

With this kind of rough life, how does a lineman get into the Hall of Fame? Well, Jim Marshall did it by doing the wrong thing.

The year was 1964 and the Minnesota Vikings were going against the San Francisco 49'ers. Fran Tarkenton was the team quarterback and things were going well for the Vikings.

The score was 27-7 when Marshall's big moment came. Every lineman dreams of the day when he will pick up a loose football and run for a touchdown. He can hear the crowd cheering. He can see his name in the paper.

As Marshall came tearing through the line, his eyes flashed as wide as headlights. The ball was loose. He raked it into his arms and was off and running.

His teammates were around him screaming. The crowd was on its feet cheering. Marshall crossed the goal line with a grin like a grizzly which has found a beehive.

Then his happiness turned to pain. He realized he had run the wrong way. Marshall had run 34 yards into the San Francisco end zone. A two-point safety was given to the 49'ers.

When you visit the Hall of Fame in Canton, Ohio, look for the display with a special button. If you press it you can hear the radio broadcast of Jim Marshall scoring for the wrong team.

"Before every man there lies a wide and pleasant road that seems right but ends in death" (Prov. 14:12, TLB).

It isn't enough to mean well. Drugs may seem like fun, but they can wreck your life. Racing bikes past stop signs may seem like fun, but it can be deadly.

Life is filled with injuries caused by nice people who do the wrong thing.

God wants us to be careful. We all make mistakes. Sometimes on purpose. But He hopes we will learn what is right and work hard to do it.

1. Do you know any nice people who steal?
2. Why is God so concerned over whether we do right or wrong things?

It is easy to become confused. Help me to know the difference between right and wrong.

Olympic Decathlon champion, Bruce Jenner

three

The Impossible Goal

It could be the toughest goal in sports. Winning the Olympic decathlon demands more from a body than almost any other contest.

Decathlon means ten events. In order to be champion you must compete in all of them within two days. The athlete does not have to win each event, but he must score the highest number of total points.

On day one the athlete must run the 100-meter sprint, the long jump, shot put, high jump and 400-meter run. The next day he competes in the 110-meter high hurdles, the discus throw, pole vault, javelin and 1500-meter race.

Amazing athletes have won the decathlon. Jim Thorpe won in 1912. Bob Mathias won twice: 1948 and 1952. Rafer Johnson won in 1960; Bill Toomey, in 1968.

A young man from New York state used to think about the decathlon and dream. Bruce Jenner was a good athlete in high school. Some days he wondered what it would be like to stand on the winner's platform at the Olympics—champion of the famous decathlon; possibly the greatest athlete in the world.

One day Jenner decided to stop dreaming and start acting. It was late in life because he was already 20 years old. But he would start to train and aim for the impossible. If it took Bruce six years of hard physical sacrifice, he would pay it—to be the greatest.

Jenner changed his life to fit his goal. All of his exercise, meals, sleeping habits, hobbies—everything now had to be done with a purpose in mind: how would it help him become the champion?

In the 1972 Olympics Jenner's determination grew stronger. He not only wanted to become the decathlon champion but also to break the record. Bruce aimed at scoring more total points than any athlete in history.

The dates of July 29 and 30, 1976, became fixed in his mind. A Russian athlete, Nikolai Avilov, held the record at 8,454 points. Somehow Jenner hoped to exceed that.

The 1976 Olympics were held in Montreal. The stadium packed in 70,000 people to watch the world's greatest athletes.

Avilov, the record holder, was there. This was his third Olympics.

Fans from all over the world had traveled to cheer for their favorite. The secton from the United States was cheering loudly for Jenner. Some wore T-shirts which said, "Go Jenner Go."

Jenner's biggest two days began at 10:00 a.m. on the field. His first event was the 100-meter race. Bruce had butterflies in his stomach. Jenner finished second in the event, a good finish, earning 819 points.

After the long jump Jenner had 1,684 points. It was a long way from the record but an excellent beginning. After the shot put Jenner was in second place with 2,493 points—seven events to go.

Bruce cleared the high jump pole at 6 feet 8 inches. He now had 3,375 points. Jenner was only 69 points out of first place.

After the 400-meter race Jenner was in a good position. He had won the race and at the end of the day had 4,298 points—35 away from first place.

Jenner felt good. He had no doubt he could close the gap on the second day. His strongest events were yet to come.

July 30 started badly. Jenner didn't finish well in the high hurdles. He was now 90 points out of first place. Bruce had expected to be closer by now.

In the discus throw he scored big and moved into second place. He was now only 9 points out of first. With three events left Jenner had regained his confidence.

Bruce sailed over with the pole vault at 15.9 and moved into first place. He now led by 66 points.

The javelin throw wasn't difficult for Jenner. His longest throw was 224 feet, 10 inches. He now held on to first place by nearly 200 points. The American was almost certainly the decathlon champion.

But there was that other record. The one he dreamed about. Could he become the highest point scorer of all time? Many ath-

letes had said 8,500 points were probably as many as any athlete could ever reach. Jenner now had a chance to go over that mark.

The 1500-meter race was the last event standing between him and the championship. (This race is just 359 feet short of a mile.)

Jenner came in a tight second but with enough points to shatter the old record. He had scored an amazing 8,618 points. At that moment he may have been the greatest athlete in the world.

Bruce Jenner wanted the decathlon so badly he even surprised himself. For six years he had put aside everything that could hurt him. In the end it paid off.

It is hard to imagine what people can do with this type of dedication. Many of us stumble and fall in life because we let sins tie us up.

"Let us strip off anything that slows us down or holds us back, and especially those sins that wrap themselves so tightly around our feet and trip us up; and let us run with patience the particular race that God has set before us" (Heb. 12:1, TLB).

What would you like to be in life? A doctor, lawyer, mechanic, athlete, missionary, an entertainer? Whatever it is, you can do it better with a clear head and a healthy body. Too many foolish people have wrecked themselves because they weren't careful to keep their body and soul clean.

1. How many events are in the decathlon?
2. How many points did Bruce Jenner score?

Help us drop off the things which hurt us.

four

The Ex-Con

Ron LeFlore was going nowhere. When he was in the sixth grade he was a thief. As a teenager he spent 18 months in the state reformatory. At 19 he was arrested for armed robbery. Ron LeFlore was going nowhere.

By this time he looked like an incurable crook. The judge could have sentenced Ron to 40 years in prison. Because of his age and his parents' pleading, the sentence was reduced to 5 to 15 years. He was sent to the State Prison in Jackson, Michigan.

Prison was a miserable place for LeFlore, as it is for most people. A convict never knew when he might be attacked or beaten up. Inmates became hardened and couldn't trust each other.

Each convict lives in a cell by himself at Jackson. It is only 2 yards wide and 10 feet long. It has a small bed, a toilet, sink, desk and locker. Before long it feels like a shoe box.

Sometimes LeFlore was put into solitary confinement. These cells were just as small and all they had was a toilet, sink and bed. There was no mattress or sheets—just two government blankets. Prisoners were not allowed to talk to anyone except two visitors a month. Convicts had to go to solitary confinement if they broke the prison rules. LeFlore was still trying to act tough and had to go there several times.

To give himself something to do Ron spent some time playing sports. First he tried basketball and did better than he expected. Someone saw the way he handled the ball and asked him to give baseball a try.

Detroit Tigers centerfielder Ron LeFlore slides safely into third under the tag of Wayne Gross of the Oakland A's.

Why not? Prison was dull and boring. At the rate he was going he would have to spend more than his five years there. Maybe baseball would be a good way to kill time. He noticed ball players got out of their cell more often. They also seemed to be treated better by the other inmates.

LeFlore had been a youth of the streets. His idea of sport was shoplifting or running from the police. He had played almost no baseball, but he would try.

In the spring of 1971 he tried out for the baseball team. He had never hit a real baseball before. Ron made the team. His fellow players were all robbers and murderers.

LeFlore was so good everyone mentioned it. He was also fast. Ron could run the 100-yard dash in 9.6 seconds.

Word finally got to the Detroit Tigers about the ball-playing prisoner. At first they weren't interested. After being asked several times, the management agreed to talk to LeFlore. He had spent three years in jail and could be paroled soon. In May of 1973 manager Billy Martin and others came to see him.

The Detroit Tigers had signed a convict before. Gates Brown came from an Ohio prison. He turned out to be a fantastic pinch hitter.

After they saw LeFlore play, the Tigers signed him. He was told to report to Clinton, Iowa, after his parole. The next year he joined the Detroit team late in the season. A little over a year before, he had been a convict in the Jackson prison.

LeFlore's first full year with the Tigers was good. His next two years were outstanding. In 1976 he batted .316. In 1977 he batted .325.

Ron was off to a great start. He not only batted and fielded well but led the league in stolen bases. He was still stealing, but now he kept it on the baseball field.

LeFlore started his life like so many other young people. He lived in a tough neighborhood and ran around with the wrong crowd. Fortunately, his life turned around and baseball was a great help.

It isn't too late for any young person. They get into trouble. They often want to turn around but don't think they can. Ron LeFlore is a good reason to hope.

"When someone becomes a Christian he becomes a brand new person inside. He is not the same any more. A new life has begun!" (2 Cor. 5:17, TLB).

Jesus Christ wants to help us change our lives. He can do more than sports, jobs or even friends. He is willing to give us a new hope and a new life. Christ has been changing people for centuries.

1. Why was LeFlore arrested?
2. How fast did he run in prison?

No one is hopeless in Jesus Christ.

five

Double Eagle II

If you think school is dull, try ballooning for a little excitement. Not just regular ballooning, but how about a trip across the Atlantic Ocean? Learn about it before you go. It could be more adventure than you want.

Men have been riding under balloons for 200 years. For the past hundred they have been trying to cross the ocean. In August of 1978 three men finally made the amazing, dangerous trip.

The balloon was called the Double Eagle II. It would climb as high as 24,000 feet into the sky. The "ship" is kept aloft by helium gas. When they wanted to fly lower they simply released helium from the balloon.

Despite the dangers, men keep sailing in balloons. Many (1,200) people have them for sport. They can be terrifically expensive ($30,000+).

Some men have died trying to cross the Atlantic. Others have nearly frozen to death. Several have said they would never try it again.

The trip is long and expensive. The men spent 137 hours and 3 minutes in the air. Total cost was more than $125,000.

A large box was tied to the bottom of the balloon and served as home for six days. Called a gondola, it measured six feet by eight feet. The close space was crowded with food, radio equipment and clothing. It also carried a sail in case the gondola needed to become a boat in a hurry.

The three men who piloted this craft knew exactly what they were doing—even down to the paint colors. They painted the top of the balloon a shiny silver. This would make the sun rays bounce off. If the balloon became too hot, it would expand and go up. They painted the bottom black. This color collects heat from the ocean. If the bottom half cooled too much, the vessel would start going down.

The entire trip was dangerous. One problem was the lack of oxygen. At certain heights the men needed to wear masks to help them breathe. They were hard to get used to and made sleeping difficult.

If the breathing didn't bother them, the temperature did. Some nights it dropped to eight degrees. They were fortunate; it could have gotten much colder.

At first it was hard to sleep. The men didn't know what they might face when they woke up. Maybe they would be crashing. Possibly their oxygen would be cut off. Naturally, one of the three was always on watch.

How does anyone steer a balloon? There is no wheel to turn or stick to push. In many ways a balloon is at the mercy of the wind. The crew can make the vessel go lower by releasing helium. They can make it go higher by throwing off weights. But this is all they can do. How fast and what direction is entirely up to the wind streams.

A wind stream will carry the balloon for so far. Then the vessel is stranded. The crew then needs to raise or lower the balloon until they find another current. They then ride it as far as it will go.

They carry weights especially for raising the balloon. The Double Eagle II was loaded with 4,000 pounds of sand bags and potatoes. These weights are called ballasts.

Probably the most dangerous part of the trip came near Ireland. The balloon was riding at the 24,000-foot level. Suddenly it started to drop like a rock—20,000, 18,000, 16,000.

The crew began throwing weights over, but the vessel kept dropping—14,000, 12,000. They were getting low on sandbags. They knew they didn't dare throw all of them out. (One balloon trip failed just because they ran out of ballasts.) It was still dropping—10,000, 8,000.

It looked as if their balloon would drop into the ocean—6,000 feet! The men started throwing radio equipment and clothing overboard. Next came the floor boards. 4,000 feet! They cut loose the hang glider which they had carried.

Finally it began to rise. Soon they settled down gently in a farmer's field in Miserey, France.

The three-man crew completed one of the most amazing flights in history. They guided a balloon, which was almost impossible to guide, and took it across the Atlantic Ocean.

Everything needs some way to steer. It needs a wheel, a stick, a rudder, ballasts or something. Otherwise the results could be disastrous. People are the same way. Without some kind of a guide our life could end up with some tragic mistakes.

"I will instruct you (says the Lord) and guide you along the best pathway for your life; I will advise you and watch your progress" (Ps. 32:8, TLB).

A smart person keeps his lines open with God. Not that He wants to take all the decisions away from us. He just wants to offer some guidance. It could save us from some "wrecks" in life.

1. How high did the balloon go?
2. Why did they tear up the floor boards?

We can guide ourselves only so much—we need good direction.

six

The Greatest Woman Athlete

It didn't look as if she had much of a career in sports. To begin with, she was a woman. They were supposed to cook and sew. There wasn't room in the world of athletics for women.

If this wasn't enough of a problem, there was her size. She barely reached 5 feet head to toe. Maybe she should find an easier job.

Babe Didrikson Zaharias was too good an athlete to give up. When she first went out for girls' basketball at her high school, she was turned down. Too short. Determined to make it, Babe practiced on her own and received special help from the boys' coach.

Not only did she make the girls' team, but she reached the biggest honor of them all. In 1950 a newspaper poll named her the best woman athlete of the past 50 years.

When they finally let her play, Babe outplayed everybody. Her high school team won the state championship. She soon started to play for an insurance company. For three straight years she was named All-American. During one game she did the nearly impossible: Babe scored 108 points.

Basketball wasn't to be her only sport. Eventually she took up bowling, baseball, tennis, javelin throwing, golf, swimming and running. She became a champion at all of them.

Babe never wanted to be half a competitor. She enjoyed sports so much she tried everything. When a track meet was announced she signed up. How many events were there going to be? Ten. She entered all of them. But she couldn't win at everything. That day she only won 8 of the 10.

At the age of 18 Babe entered the 1932 Olympics. She performed so well she was named Woman Athlete of the Year. She was an encouragement to women around the world. Now they, too, had an athlete whom they could admire.

Babe wanted to play baseball but there weren't many women's teams as good as she was. That couldn't stop her. She joined a men's team. They traveled around the nation.

In 1934 Babe had a chance to pitch for one inning against a professional baseball team. The Philadelphia Athletics sent their best up to face her. They were able to get hits but couldn't score. We will never know how she would have done as a major league player. She might have made it.

When Babe tackled the game of golf, she put everything she had into it. Some days she would practice until her hands bled. Naturally she became the world's greatest woman golfer. Babe won 17 major golf tournaments in a row. She won 50 tournaments altogether.

Babe wasn't happy to stay an amateur. When she turned to professional sports, she won practically every event open to women. As a professional golfer she became a very wealthy woman.

Like most athletes Babe was healthy and feeling great. One sports writer called her the greatest athlete alive—man or woman. But she couldn't tell how long she might have to live.

Cancer had entered her body. They operated but it came back. The strong life of a fantastic athlete ended at 42.

Many athletes die as young adults—Lou Gehrig, Brian Piccalo. Good health is no guarantee. Life doesn't consist of how many years we have—only what we do with those years.

"Living or dying we follow the Lord. Either way we are his" (Rom. 14:8, TLB).

We can live those years with Jesus Christ. As a follower of His, every year can be lived to its best.

1. How tall was Babe?
2. How many golf tournaments did she win in a row?

Life flies by too fast to waste it by doing evil.

seven

The First Black Player

Jackie Robinson was one of the best athletes and bravest men who ever played baseball. He was one of those rare stars who could have been either a professional baseball player or a football champion. While a student in California he was named an All-American as a running back.

His decision to be a baseball player may have seemed foolish to some. Robinson was a black man and no one of his race was allowed to play in the major leagues.

But Robinson picked up his courage and was determined to make it. One day Branch Rickey gave him a call. Would Jackie be willing to give it a try with the Brooklyn Dodgers? It wouldn't be a hard decision to make. This was the day he had dreamed of.

During the late 1940's people were slow to accept a black man in baseball. In some towns where he played, the crowds booed Robinson and called him names. People would throw cups and sometimes bottles when he went to bat.

The baseball players on other teams often treated him badly. Even a few members of his own team refused to talk to Jackie unless it was to call him names.

But Robinson kept up his courage. Some days it was hard. Once in a while a fight broke out on the team. But still he did a remarkable job. He not only made the team, but Jackie also was an exciting star to watch.

One day was particularly hard for the first black star. He was playing second base in Ebbets Field when a member of the other team hit a ball into right field. The runner rounded first base and darted for second in what looked like a close play.

The right fielder came up with the ball and threw a fast shot to second. Robinson took the ball just in time to whirl and tag out the runner. Seeing he was too late, the batter lifted his spikes and pushed them into Robinson's chest.

Furious, Jackie hit the runner in the face with the ball. In a second they were going at it in a fierce fight. Players started to come out of the dugouts, but the umpires quickly calmed things down.

Members of the opposing team began calling Robinson ugly names. The fans soon joined in the shouting match. Cups, bottles and wrappers came flying out of the seats in Robinson's direction. The field was being covered with trash.

The man who played shortstop next to Robinson was a Kentuckian named PeeWee Reese—a short fellow and excellent ball player. Suddenly, he raised his hands and called time out.

PeeWee walked over to Robinson. With the crowd still booing, Reese put his arm around Jackie and the two stood there for a long silent moment.

Reese showed a great deal of courage to let a friend know he could count on him. It wasn't an easy time to stick his neck out, but PeeWee had to help a lonely friend.

"There are 'friends' who pretend to be friends, but there is a friend who sticks closer than a brother" (Prov. 18:24, TLB).

Christ helped many people who were "different." Some were of different races and Jesus visited in their homes. Others had diseases but Christ ate with them. Some were just not popular, but Jesus worked by their sides.

Some people didn't like Jesus Christ because He was "different." But the Son of God loved all kinds.

1. Why do people dislike those of other races?
2. Have you ever helped someone who was being treated badly?

Jesus said He is my friend. Help me to be a good friend when my buddies need me.

eight

Jim Zorn
Takes a Risk

Young people from all over are collecting pictures of famous athletes. In our house we have autographed photos from Vince Ferragamo, O. J. Simpson and Roger Staubach.

When you are an outstanding athlete, thousands of young people watch your every step. Many want to grow up to be just like you. They notice if their hero smokes, swears, and how he talks to referees.

Most athletes are careful to be good examples. Some of them openly discuss their Christian faith.

We recently received an autographed picture from Jim Zorn, quarterback for the Seattle Seahawks. He not only signed his name but also wrote the references to two Bible verses.

Zorn took a stand. He says he is a Christian. Now people will watch him to see if he lives like one.

Zorn's football career is going well. In 1978 the Associated Press named him the second string all-pro quarterback behind Terry Bradshaw. The Seahawks almost made the play-off that year and have a bright future.

This young star started off the hard way. In 1975 he almost made the Dallas Cowboys. Just before their first game he was dropped. Zorn stayed out of football that year but tried the next season with the Seahawks. Now he is the town hero.

When Zorn isn't playing football he likes to speed skate, box and juggle. The rest of the time he shares his Christian testimony at groups, banquets and with individuals.

Maybe Zorn will someday make a big mistake. He might say

or do something which will not seem Christian. But he seems to realize that you don't have to be perfect. Christians are people who believe Jesus Christ died for their sins. Jim Zorn is willing to let anyone know he belongs to Christ.

One of the Bible references on Zorn's picture is 1 Corinthians 1:31:

"If anyone is going to boast, let him boast only of what the Lord has done" (TLB).

1. What team dropped Zorn?
2. What are Zorn's hobbies?

We are glad people tell about their Christian faith.

Jim Zorn, Seattle Seahawks quarterback sets up a running play.

nine

Championship at Last

E lvin Hayes didn't start out as an outstanding basketball player. In his early years he helped pick cotton in the South. Imagine how hard he found it to pick cotton when he was 6 feet 9 1/2 inches tall.

Basketballs felt more comfortable in his hands. By the time he was in high school everyone could see he was different. Elvin was the star of the Eula Britton High School team. He gained national attention in his senior year when the team won 54 games in a row. During that season he averaged 35 points per game.

The University of Houston soon grabbed Hayes up and he spent four outstanding years there. In his next to last year, Houston played UCLA for the national championship.

Two fantastic athletes were meeting on the court. UCLA had Kareem Abdul-Jabbar, who later became a professional star. The California team had won 47 games in a row. Both men played well, with Hayes out-scoring Abdul-Jabbar.

In the last seconds of the game Elvin Hayes was fouled and came to the line to shoot. The score was 69-69. He had already posted 39 points. But Hayes wasn't a great foul shooter. Could he make these two? The first shot dropped straight in. The second shot looked like its twin brother. Houston won the championship 71-69.

It is difficult to be a college athlete. It is even harder to make it professionally. Hayes decided to try and joined the San Diego Rockets.

During Hayes' first ten years of professional basketball his statistics were amazing. Every year he was selected for the All-Star Team. During those ten years, he played 887 games and missed five. One year Elvin led the league in scoring and twice in rebounds. Those ten years he moved among the best stars in basketball history. He became the 10th highest scorer of all time, averaging 23.9 points per game. Only six players have caught more rebounds than the former cotton picker.

For all of his ability yet there was one goal that seemed to elude him. Hayes had played on a championship team in high school. His college team had won the National Championship. But he had never been on a professional championship team. Elvin wanted the chance to win it all.

He had moved to the Washington Bullets and they were an excellent team. In 1972 they went to the playoffs but lost to the New York Knicks.

In 1973 they went to the playoffs again. The Knicks shut them down again.

In 1974 the Bullets reached the finals. The Golden State Warriors took them four straight.

Year after year it was the same story. They could make the playoffs but couldn't seem to win the big one. Some people compared them to football's Minnesota Vikings.

When a team comes close year after year and doesn't win it, fans, management and players start getting upset. Whose fault was it? Many people started blaming Hayes. They said he choked up when the big games came along. This really bothered the outstanding star. He wanted that championship more than anything.

In June, 1978, they went for the top prize again. This time their opponent was the Seattle Supersonics. For seven hard-fought games the two teams locked horns. When the final buzzer sounded, the Washington Bullets were winners. After ten seasons Elvin Hayes had his championship.

Hayes had a great desire to be a winner. He stuck with it and his dream came true. The Apostle Paul wanted to be a winner also. Not on the athletic field but in the Christian life. He worked as hard as any athlete to try to be like Jesus Christ.

"I strain to reach the end of the race and receive the prize for which God is calling us up to heaven because of what Christ Jesus did for us" (Phil. 3:14, TLB).

Paul tried to keep his life clean—not just by what he ate and drank; not just by exercising. He also tried to keep hate, jealousy and selfishness out.

It was hard to try to become more like Christ. But Paul was going to be a winner—whatever it cost him.

1. In his first ten years, how often was Hayes named to All-Star?
2. How many games did Hayes' high school team win in a row?

Let's run the race to win.

ten

The "Confused" Baseball Player

There are so many rules in sports it is easy to get confused. The infield fly rule is hard to remember. If an outfielder catches a ball and falls over the fence, is it an out or a home run?

One of the most confusing plays happened in the early days of baseball. It was so surprising few people have done it since.

The main character was a pitcher named Jimmy St. Vrain. He played for the Chicago Cubs and joined the major leagues as a teenager. Jimmy was an excellent pitcher and it looked as if he would have a long career.

Pitchers have always had one problem, though. They spend so much time practicing pitching, they are often terrible batters. This may not be true for children, but in the major leagues it can be a big problem. This is why the Designated Hitter was introduced.

This pitcher looked as if he had never tried batting. When he went to the plate it was embarrassing. He would take a wide, wild swing and miss the ball altogether.

When Jimmy batted, you could always count on one easy out every nine men up.

Batting practice didn't seem to help. The manager was desperate. If only Jimmy could hit the ball, it would help move the players to the next base.

Finally the manager thought of a solution.

"Jimmy, I want you to try something different," the manager said.

"What's the use? I just can't hit it," said Jimmy, sadly.

"Maybe the problem is that you are swinging the wrong way. You pitch with your left hand but bat right-handed. Why don't we turn you around and let you bat left-handed too?"

It was worth a try. What did they have to lose?

The next time up St. Vrain went to the plate and stood on the other side. It felt funny to swing this way but he was going to do it.

A fast ball came whipping past and Jimmy just stood there. The opposing team was relaxed. They could see an easy out coming.

The second pitch came whipping toward the plate. Smack! Jimmy hit it solidly. The ball took two big bounces toward the shortstop. The fielder picked up the ball and started to throw it to first. Suddenly he stopped.

St. Vrain was running with all his might. In his excitement he was running toward third base.

With a big smile the shortstop tossed the ball toward first. Jimmy was out by a whole ball field.

He never did become a big hitting star but he did hit the ball. Jimmy even learned which base to run to.

It is easy to become confused. There is so much to know. We get advice from so many places, we often don't know what to do.

There is no reason to be confused about God. He wants us to know who He is and what He is like. The best place to find out is in the pages of the Bible.

"For God is not the author of confusion, but of peace, as in all churches of the saints" (1 Cor. 14:33, KJV).

Many religous groups are working hard to sell their idea of God. Some of them are cults and are even dangerous. Young people often turn to them because they are confused about God. The Bible will give us a description of a loving, understanding, forgiving God.

1. Whom did Jimmy St. Vrain play for?
2. What is God like? Explain.

Thanks for showing us what God is like in Jesus Christ.

eleven

The Greatest Athlete?

Everyone has a favorite sports figure. Many people feel the greatest athlete of this century was a Sac-Fox Indian named Jim Thorpe. In 1950 a major magazine named him the best athlete of the past 50 years.

Thorpe was a college star at Carlisle Indian School, a 1912 Olympic champion, a professional baseball player and for 12 years the biggest name in football.

In the early days football was played mostly in small towns like Canton, Ohio. As a struggling sport it needed a name player who could draw crowds. Thorpe had become famous across the nation because of his victories in the Olympics.

He was hired by the Canton Bulldogs to be their player-coach. His total salary was $250 a game. Thorpe was a real bargain. He would put on a show to excite any sports fan.

As a runner Thorpe was almost unstoppable. The famous Knute Rockne teased him during one game that he could stop the strong star. Thorpe ran over Rockne and raced 60 yards for a touchdown. It took several people to help Rockne off the field.

When his team didn't have the ball, Thorpe played defensive lineman. Runners hated to get tackled by him. He would roll over the player's legs and crush them with tremendous force.

Red Grange later made football the big sport it is today. But in those early years, Thorpe furnished the headlines. For a short time he served as president of the football league.

Today there is an excellent statue of Thorpe in the Football Hall of Fame. In the entrance the first thing a visitor sees is the

Jim Thorpe was a great star in many sports, including college and professional football.

form of Thorpe holding a football, racing full speed.

But not all of Thorpe's sports days were happy ones. In his early career he didn't understand many of the rules and broke an important one.

Thorpe had been a star of the 1912 Olympics held in Stockholm. He was a gold medal winner and was invited to meet the king of Sweden.

The Olympics are contests held solely for amateurs. They can never have received pay for playing sports. After the Olympics it was discovered that Thorpe had played one summer of baseball while in college. He was paid just a few dollars for each game and Thorpe never thought much of it.

When the Olympic committee heard about this, they voted to take back his medals. It is difficult to imagine the heartbreak. To Thorpe's credit he went on still to become an outstanding professional athlete.

"Follow the Lord's rules for doing his work, just as an athlete either follows the rules or is disqualified and wins no prize" (2 Tim. 2:5, TLB).

There was once a little boy who stole some money to help feed a poor family. He did a wonderful thing, but he went about it in the wrong way. When his parents found out, his happiness turned to sadness.

God gave us rules to live by. The Ten Commandments are some of those rules. When we break them we hurt ourselves, sometimes our friends and sometimes our parents. We also hurt God because He was hoping so hard we would do what was right.

1. Why do people dislike rules?
2. Can you name some good rules?

Thank you, Lord, for cheering for me. You want to see me get the most out of life by keeping the rules.

twelve

America's Father of Soccer

Soccer is one of the fastest growing sports in the United States. Young people play it in school yards and on back lots all over the country. Though it has been played for years, only recently has it become a big sport.

Many people like the game because it is so easy to get a match going. There is little expense since the only equipment needed is a ball. It is a fast game where even the lesser athletes get a chance to play. There is a great deal of running to help build up the legs and body.

Soccer had been a popular sport in Europe and South America but had never been a big professional event in the United States. Teams were formed but few people came to see them. They lost money year after year.

Then the New York Cosmos soccer team came up with a brilliant idea. Why not hire a star player from another country? He could add more excitement to the game and start people talking about soccer.

The man they had in mind was from Brazil. His name was Pelé. At the age of 34 he retired after being a famous star. His South American team had won three world championships.

To get this superstar out of retirement, the Cosmos paid Pelé almost five million dollars to play three years. This made the speedy athlete the highest paid in the world.

Pelé became an instant star in the United States. No longer were one or two thousand people showing up for a game. It wasn't uncommon for 30,000 fans to show. When the Fort Lauderdale

Pelé, who has played in Brazil and the United States, is the most famous soccer player in the world.

Strikers and the New York Cosmos played in 1977, over 77,000 people bought tickets.

The sport was appealing to people of all ages. Almost half of the audiences were women who enjoyed soccer.

Other stars had come from Europe and South America, but quickly the game was changing. The U.S. players were soon becoming stars. Thanks to Pelé, soccer was about to be an American sport.

If 1977 was to be his last year, Pelé wanted to go out a winner. After a tough fight for the top, Soccer Bowl-77 was finally played. The Cosmos beat the Seattle Sounders 2-1.

When Pelé and his teammates returned to the New York airport, 5,000 people met them. Soccer had become a major sport in America. Pelé went back home to Brazil knowing he had been a good father.

Leaders are great if you get the right ones. The Cosmos picked a good star in Pelé. But many people pick some strange leaders to follow.

It isn't uncommon to see a good young person get into trouble tagging behind the wrong friend. They start doing things they otherwise would never do.

All of us have people we respect, friends we would enjoy being like. But if we aren't careful, we may pick someone who will only lead us into trouble. That person may be a good friend, but in the long run we are going to be sorry.

The most dependable leader in the world is Jesus Christ. He is worth believing in and following. When we put him in command of our life, we can select our friends much better.

"For his suffering made Jesus a perfect Leader; one fit to bring them into their salvation" (Heb. 2:10, TLB).

1. Who are the two people you most enjoy being with?
2. How does Jesus Christ make a good leader?

I need to decide that Jesus will be the leader of my life.

thirteen

Pictures on the Wall

He was a dirty man dressed in an old, baggy suit. His shirt used to be white and his tie had lost its color.

A couple of times each week we would see him walking in the halls near the high school gym. He would stop and look at the pictures mounted on the wall. The pictures were old, some of them 50 years old.

They were photographs of best athletes to play at Eastern High. Some held all-city track records, others played football in outstanding colleges. We used to look at them and dream what it would be like to have our picture hanging there.

One day we were talking to the coach when the odd-looking man was wandering in the hall. Coach told us the story.

The man's name was Mike Hanson and he had attended Eastern. It had been 25 years ago, but during his day he was a star athlete. He had broken several track and field records. For a quarter century one of those records still remained unbroken.

Hanson was so good that his picture was hanging on the wall. He came regularly to check on it.

On graduation night this young man, filled with energy and a bright future, decided to celebrate. He drove the car and someone else provided the alcohol. After a fast evening of drinking and parties, Mike and his five friends piled into the car and took to the highway.

He rounded the curves until the last one. The car crashed like a roaring train into a telephone pole.

Doctors were able to restore Mike's body. The one who raced

like a leopard and leaped like a gazelle was saved. But Mike's mind never worked the same again.

Now his life was reduced to walking the streets and the school hall. His eyes tried to focus, but you could tell he didn't see correctly.

As he stared at his own picture, he fought to remember. He tried to recall the crowds, the newspaper stories and the trophies. But the rest of his life he will only look back and try to remember.

Mike Hanson was a healthy young man who had a great chance for a happy life. Just a few minutes of foolishness sent him into years of sad confusion.

Accidents can happen to anyone. No one wants to just sit home because he might get hurt if he goes out. But we are fools if we cloud up our minds by getting drunk. It may sound like fun, but too many people get hurt and some never get over it.

"Wine gives false courage; hard liquor leads to brawls; what fools men are to let it master them, making them reel drunkenly down the streets!" (Prov. 20:1, TLB).

1. Name one foolish thing you did and are sorry for.
2. What attitude should you take toward alcohol?

Life is packed with good days. Guide me so I will not confuse my mind with alcohol and drugs.

fourteen

What a Hitting Streak!

The great batter, Ted Williams, said the hardest thing in sports is to hit a baseball. It certainly is one of the most difficult.

A good fastball pitcher may throw over 100 miles per hour. A batter has to take a round stick and hit it.

No one did this better than an outfielder from San Francisco named Joe DiMaggio. He played for 13 years in New York City and was called the Yankee Clipper. During that time the Yankees played in ten World Series and won nine of them.

Two famous batters had a great year in 1941. They were Ted Williams and Joe DiMaggio. Williams played for Boston and hit an average of .406 for the season. So far no one else has done that in the 38 years that have passed.

But DiMaggio did an even more amazing thing that year. Early in the season the young "Clipper" got hot at the bat. He hit in game after game. Soon he went 20 games straight and got a hit in every game. Then in 25 games he still had at least one hit each game.

As summer turned into late June people everywhere were talking. DiMaggio had gone 35 games and still had a hit in each one.

Soon it was no longer interesting just to New York fans. Newspapers carried the story in small towns all over America. July came. He passed 40 games. How long could it last?

The pressure got stronger. What day would DiMaggio finally go without a hit? Who would be the pitcher to stop him? Or

Joe DiMaggio raps out a home run during the season he hit safely 56 games in a row.

could the young star go the entire season and get a hit every game? People packed into ball parks wherever the Yankees played.

July kept rolling and so did DiMaggio. It became 45, 47, 49 and then 50. Reporters were always crowding him with questions. What did it feel like? How long could he do it? Were the pitchers letting him hit the ball?

But pitchers were eager to get him out. They wanted to be the one who stopped the Yankee Clipper. The games rolled by—52, 54, 55.

In 1941 there were only 154 games in a season. When DiMaggio hit safely in 56 games in a row, that made over one-third of the entire season.

Baseball has many great names—Cobb, Ruth, Hornsby, Gehrig. But no one has ever done this.

On July 17, 1941, the answer finally came. The place was Cleveland and the crowd came to see baseball's amazing hitter. On that day two pitchers, Al Smith and Jim Bagby, closed the door. DiMaggio couldn't get a safe hit and his streak ended at 56.

Many records have come and gone. Sooner or later someone breaks them. But if there is one record which may never be beaten, it is this one. DiMaggio was a steady hitter longer than anyone who ever played the game.

"All our greatness is like a flower that droops and falls; but the Word of the Lord will last forever" (1 Pet. 1:24, 25, TLB).

People do amazing things in the world of sports. But even the greatest only last for a while. They grow old and have to stop playing. Sooner or later most of the records are broken by a younger person.

Only God and His love last forever. It has never struck out or had a losing season. Athletics are fun for now. We can put our trust in God forever.

1. Would you like to live forever? Why?
2. If God will live forever, where do you think He came from?

Make me a fan who cheers for a great God.

fifteen

Paul, the Sports Fan

The famous apostle Paul must have been enthused about sports. Several times he uses illustrations in the Bible which describe athletic contests.

During Paul's day neither baseball, football nor basketball was around. People enjoyed their sports from field, track and wrestling.

The most famous events were the Olympics. They were held every four years and had gone on for hundreds of years.

At first only men were allowed to compete in the Olympics, but later it was changed to include boys.

Before anyone could participate he had to take a special oath. First, he had to say he had trained for at least ten months. Second, he had to promise not to cheat in any way. If these oaths were not kept, the person had to pay a heavy fine and he became a disgrace to his home country.

The events could include running, discus and spear throwing, wrestling, boxing, chariot racing and running in full armor.

Sometimes valuable prizes were awarded to winners, but often only crowns were given. These crowns consisted of leaves and would shortly dry up. The real honor came when the athlete returned home.

At Athens the victors received a large financial gift in a public ceremony. From then on he was given a special seat for all the local athletic contests.

Sports were extremely popular in Israel during Paul's life. They were probably talked about in the same way they are today.

King Herod enjoyed the games and had special theaters built in Caesarea and Jerusalem for athletic contests. Sports had been in poor condition when he helped rebuild their popularity.

Paul was also aware of athletic contests between men and animals. An armed man might have to fight a gigantic lion. The crowds cheered. Often the man was killed (1 Cor. 15:32).

The apostle often talked about athletics because he knew people enjoyed them. When he wrote to the Greek town of Corinth, Paul compared the Christian life with the sports contests.

"In a race, everyone runs but only one person gets first prize. So run your race to win. To win the contest you must deny yourselves many things that keep you from doing your best. An athlete goes to all this trouble just to win a blue ribbon or a silver cup, but we do it for a heavenly reward that never disappears. So I run straight to the goal with purpose in every step. I fight to win. I'm not just shadow-boxing or playing around. Like an athlete I punish my body, treating it roughly, training it to do what it should, not what it wants to. Otherwise I fear that after enlisting others for the race, I myself might be declared unfit and ordered to stand aside" (1 Cor. 9:24-27, TLB).

Paul was aware of the Olympic rules and knew his readers would be also. The steady Christian life took as much dedication as any athletic contest. He knew people dare not follow Christ lightly.

1. In what sport have you practiced and become better? Explain.
2. How can you "practice" being a Christian?

It is hard to live like a Christian unless we do it regularly.

sixteen

Parachuting for Sport

Who was the first person to sail through the air with a parachute? One thing for certain, it happened long before the first airplane flew.

One of the oldest pictures of a parachute was drawn by Leonardi da Vinci in 1495. We don't know if he ever tried one but we know he could have.

The first parachute jump which can be definitely proven happened 300 years later. André Garnerin held a show in Paris in 1797. He announced he would jump from a balloon using a parachute. Thousands came to see the wild adventure. It must have been as exciting as seeing a man go to the moon.

Men tried to improve parachutes and began jumping from greater heights. In 1837 the first man was killed while trying to jump 5,000 feet.

Parachuting has come a long way and has developed into an exciting sport. The first people to do it just for the fun of it were the Russians in the 1930's. They formed clubs, practiced and put on shows.

During World War II the parachute played an important role. It is given credit for saving over 100,000 lives. At least one man was saved four times but was killed the fifth.

Parachuting has come a long way since the early days of 2,000 to 3,000 foot jumps. Some jumps have been made from over 100,000 feet. For most of the distances a person will "free-fall" without opening his parachute. If he jumps from this height at around 90,000 feet, his body will be traveling at 750 miles per hour.

Nick Piantanida was one of the first men to jump from this height. He did it three times but on the third try was killed because of oxygen problems. His pressurized suit had developed mechanical difficulties.

In the early days of parachuting, it was believed that man could not "free-fall." Many thought the rush of air hitting a person would make it impossible to breathe. Today people do it regularly.

As men have felt more at home in the sky, they have tried more daring adventures. Some years ago a man decided to try a stunt which would amaze everyone. He jumped out of an airplane without a parachute.

Two of his friends caught up with him in air and handed him a chute. While still falling he put the parachute on, tied it and pulled the cord. He floated safely to the ground.

While it was exciting, the stunt was also illegal. The men had to pay thousands of dollars in fines to the government.

Men's and women's groups compete for national championships every year. There is also a world championship program where countries are matched against each other. The events include trying to land in a drawn circle, style of parachuting and overall ability.

Today there are probably 40,000 people who parachute just for the fun of it. Each year over two million jumps are made.

In 1974 a world's record was set when 31 men joined in a "free-fall." They all held hands in a giant circle and "fell" before opening their parachutes. By now this record has probably been broken.

A man in California is trying to make it possible for practically everyone to parachute. He has built a small go-cart with a chute attached. The wind will pick up the person, go-cart and all, and carry him in the air at about 25 miles per hour. When the passenger gets to his place, he merely lowers the craft and walks into his office or home.

One of the most interesting jumpers was "Batman" Clem Sohn. He would dive from an airplane at 20,000 feet wearing a suit of canvas wings. They allowed Sohn to "fly." It was an amazing stunt and must have felt exciting. At around 1,000 feet he would open his parachute and sail safely to the ground. In 1937 neither of his chutes opened and he plunged to his death.

Not many people are killed parachuting. Thousands do it safely every year. Parachutists take special care and use two chutes to make sure nothing will go wrong.

They listen to the instructions and note all the warnings. But if the warnings are ignored, it can turn into an extremely dangerous sport.

All of life is this way. When we listen to the danger signals and are careful, it is a much better world. This is one of the reasons God gave us the Bible.

"I am not writing about these things to make you ashamed, but to warn and counsel you as beloved children" (1 Cor. 4:14, TLB).

Life can be fun, interesting, even exciting. But those who laugh at the warnings often get hurt and hurt other people. God has given us guidance and warnings in the Scriptures. The wise youth learns them, keeps them and enjoys life.

1. When did Leonardi da Vinci draw a parachute?
2. Why did the government fine a parachutist?

The first step to enjoying life is to listen to God.

seventeen

The Problem with Heroes

Television brings sports heroes into our homes every week. It's really fun to watch them there as well as at the ball park.

There is excitement in watching a crafty runner steal home with two out in the ninth, like Jackie Robinson used to do. It's fun to see Fran Tarkenton scramble around with four Pittsburgh Steelers trying to jump him. It's a thrill to watch Bill Walton shoot down the Philadelphia 76'ers for the basketball championship.

It's good to view athletes we can look up to and even admire. But sometimes we are tempted to put athletes on too high a plateau. Really, they are just like everyone else. Some are kind and friendly. Others are selfish and ill-tempered.

There was once a great baseball player who became famous across the country. Children and adults read about him daily and bought whatever he advertised. In his personal life he was a drunkard and unfaithful to his wife.

That doesn't take anything away from his ability. Sports probably never had a more natural athlete. But he also let a lot of young people down by the godless life he led.

Sports people are not the only ones who fail. Soldiers, bankers, singers—all have the same problem. They are human. They make mistakes. We should be careful not to expect too much from them.

The Washington Redskins once signed on an outstanding runner. If lightning speed ever described anyone it was this man.

67

He not only ran fast, but he also ran sideways, slicing past the linemen who were trying to stop him. He was on his way to becoming a real star.

Unfortunately, this young man was already hooked on drugs. Some days he just didn't show up for practice. Other days he was glassy-eyed and couldn't follow instructions.

Finally the ball club had to give up on him. He tried another team and then another. But his natural talent was being strangled by his personal life.

Even Christian athletes have their problems. They believe in Christ and they try to lead a steady life. But it's hard and they often have trouble. Some don't even like to say they are Christians because everyone starts picking their lives apart.

God understands that people are people whatever they do for a living. We often do wonderfully kind things, and yet sometimes we commit miserable acts.

Perhaps this is the reason King David's life story is found in the Bible. He not only did great things but he also plotted murder.

The Bible also mentions that Noah got drunk and Peter was a coward.

Heroes are fun. Everyone needs a couple of them. But don't be too disappointed if they fall on their faces once in a while. Only one person is completely dependable.

"And Christ became a human being and lived here on earth among us and was full of loving forgiveness and truth. And some of us have seen his glory—the glory of the only Son of the heavenly Father" (John 1:14, TLB).

1. Name someone close to you whom you admire. Explain why.
2. How is Jesus Christ a good example for us to follow?

Jesus Christ is the only one who is worth following completely. His behavior will never embarrass us.

eighteen

Starting Right

Everyone has to start some place. Earl Campbell decided to start on top. During his rookie year in the National Football League, he ran better than any other running back.

Every time Earl carried the ball he averaged almost 5 yards. That gave him a total of 1,450 yards. He was the first rookie to lead the league in rushing since the famous Jim Brown over 20 years before.

When the 1978 season was finished, Campbell started collecting his awards. The year before he had received the Heisman Trophy for best player in college. Now he would accept the highest honor in pro ball.

He was named Rookie of the Year. Campbell's honors went higher though. He was also selected as Player of the Year.

One person has said that Campbell is the closest thing to a locomotive on the football field. Earl is both big and fast. Tacklers seem to bounce off him, not even slowing the big Texan.

During that first season Earl took the Houston Oilers to the NFL Championship game. Pittsburgh proved too strong for the young team, but the Oilers had a big future waiting.

One of Campbell's biggest strengths was his steadiness. In seven games Earl ran for over 100 yards. When a team can count on that kind of yardage from a back, they find it much easier to win games.

Some running backs are stronger in one area than another. Maybe one is especially good at getting short yardage, like one or two yards. Others are "break away" runners. If they can get through the line, they can get the big gain. Campbell seems to do both well.

He can get the tough first down when it is needed, but he also

Houston Oilers running back Earl Campbell picks up 8 yards
against the Denver Broncos in Houston.

breaks into the open field for the long run or touchdown. He keeps the other teams guessing. They will line up to hold him on a short run and in a couple seconds he has broken loose and is heading for the end zone.

It would be easy for Campbell's teammates to become jealous of the rookie star. But according to reports they respect him because of his personality and sacrifice.

Rather than being a big bragger and "hot-dog," Earl just goes about his job. He shares the credit with his teammates. Each year that he gains 1,000 yards, he plans to take his linemen out to dinner as O. J. Simpson used to. It is a nice way of saying "thank you."

Campbell sacrifices himself for the sake of the team. If another running back is carrying the ball, he can count on the big Texan to block. He throws himself at the other team. Earl isn't tall for a pro player (5 feet 11 inches), but his 224 pounds will stop most opponents.

The Houston head coach, Bum Phillips, sees Campbell as a great team player. The team's victory comes before his personal records and the other players know it. They really want to open holes for this kind of runner.

Football fame and fortune often change players. Many think Campbell will remain "Mister Nice-Guy." Only time will tell, but he is off to a great start.

Most running backs only last four or five years before they become sidelined with a major injury. Life in pro football can really be tough. If Campbell stays healthy, friendly and fast, he just might stay on top for many years.

It is terrific to get off to a good start. Whether it is school, a job or making friends, we want to begin right. It is also important to begin early in our relationship with God. If we do, we can avoid many problems and disappointments later on.

If we learn to trust God as children, it will be easier to keep trusting Him as we grow up.

"O Lord, you alone are my hope; I've trusted you from childhood" (Ps. 71:5, TLB).

1. How many yards did Campbell gain in his rookie year?
2. How much does Campbell weigh?

It is never too early to begin trusting in God.

nineteen

Scuba Diving

Scuba diving really looks like fun. Wouldn't it be great to swim with the fish and see interesting "treasures" at the bottom of a lake or ocean? Or maybe to bring back something which has been lost underwater for years?

Scuba diving is a fast-growing sport all over the world. Millions of trained divers are swimming the shores of the United States.

Men had been trying to master the sea for a long time before scuba diving became possible. Before the time of Christ men were using a large diving "bell." It held air and allowed a person to stay under water. The diver couldn't stay long and if he went very far under, he would get terribly sick or die.

After many centuries a large diving suit was made. Air was pumped through hoses from the ship above. The person looked like a robot and was limited in his ability to move around.

Then in 1943 two Frenchmen invented our present scuba equipment. They were the famous Jacques-Yves Cousteau and Emile Gagnan. They designed the aqualung. It allowed a diver to carry air in a tank on his back.

Today it is common to see scuba divers at local lakes. Some waters are still unpolluted and clear. They make ideal locations for exploring the sea.

Don't run off and buy a suit and tank, however, and then just jump into the water. While scuba diving is fun, it can also be extremely dangerous. If it is done incorrectly, the swimmer could be hurt or killed.

Classes are available in most areas of the country.

With the correct equipment it is now possible to dive to depths of 300 feet. Some may want to spear fish, while others will take pictures, and still others will collect rocks or lost objects. Many people like to go down just to look around.

The first rule which scuba divers have learned is *never dive alone*. Too many things can go wrong. A partner may help prevent serious injury or even save a life.

There is a tremendous sense of freedom for the scuba diver. He can dive deeper, stay longer and move around more than any other form of deep swimming.

If you dive into the water and hold your breath, you can go fairly deep. In most cases 100 feet is as far as you can safely dive without an aqualung. Even then it is dangerous. After this depth the diver is taking a chance of having his chest cave in, without an aqualung.

Most divers don't go deeper than 100 feet even with special equipment. It is hard to breathe properly at this depth and most people seem to have trouble thinking clearly. Some divers become so confused they do not take steps to rescue themselves and can easily die. The ability to think will improve if a person comes up toward the surface. However, some seem unable to come up again.

Despite all these warnings, scuba diving can be an extremely safe sport. Out of the millions of dives made each year, very few people ever die from scuba diving. In the few cases when death occurs it is usually from an added factor. Maybe the diver was drinking, using drugs, or in poor physical condition.

Suppose you were diving and suddenly your air supply stopped working altogether. Even at a depth of 100 feet the *trained* scuba diver would safely and calmly rise to the surface.

Scuba diving is a great sport when it is done correctly. It can be a deadly game, though, if it isn't done right. Like the rest of life, there is a right way and a wrong way. Do what is right and you will enjoy life. Choose wrong and your life may be miserable.

For this reason God has told us to obey our parents—because it is right and right is best for us. To disobey parents can lead to hard times. The happy young person will learn to want what is right.

"Children, obey your parents; this is the right thing to do because God has placed them in authority over you" (Eph. 6:1, TLB).

1. Who invented the aqualung?
2. How deeply can man dive safely without equipment?

We suffer hard times when we ignore what is right.

twenty

Greatest Day in Track

There have been thousands of "Great Days." For centuries men have run in track meets and set amazing records. However, May 25, 1935, was a very special day, involving an outstanding athlete, Jesse Owens.

Owens grew up poor. He spent many bleak Christmases without presents since his dad was without a job. But Jesse had a great talent going for him. He was fast. Instead of feeling sorry for himself, Owens decided to use what he had to the best of his ability.

Jesse went to school in Cleveland, Ohio. As a freshman in high school he ran for the first time, covering 100 yards in 10 seconds. At the time it was astonishing. His coaches knew they had a track star.

During high school he ran 79 races. He won 75 of them.

When Owens was ready for college, the colleges were more than ready for him. Over two dozen schools offered him full scholarships to run for them.

He accepted an offer from his home state and attended Ohio State University.

Not every track meet was a big success for Owens. He had hoped to represent the U.S. in the 1932 Olympics but lost in the tryouts. He was determined to get there, though, and trained hard for the next four years.

Jesse Owens is famous for his showing in the 1936 Olympics. The Olympics were held in Berlin, with Adolph Hitler, the Nazi leader, attending—the same Hitler who later started World War II.

Hitler had said that black people were not as good as whites.

He tried to stir up one group of people against another.

When Owens went out on the field, some members of the Nazi party were in the stands. They booed Owens and the other black American athletes.

After each event Hitler shook hands with the winner. When Owens won the running jump, Hitler refused to shake his hand. Instead he congratulated the number-two man.

Owens was hurt. He had proved he was as good as anyone else. Color and race didn't make any difference.

When Jesse won the 200-meter run and set a new record, Hitler walked out. Owens probably enjoyed running Hitler off more than winning and breaking records.

But that wasn't his "great day." Owens had a greater day on the track.

While still a college student, Jesse attended a track meet in Ann Arbor, Michigan. Owens was a sick man on that day, and it looked as if he wouldn't be able to run.

However, within one hour Jesse Owens set four major track records. He became the only man in modern times to do this in one day, let alone one hour.

First came the speedy 100-yard dash. At the crack of the gun he was off and racing. He tied the then world's record at 9.4 seconds.

Just ten minutes later the call came for the running broad jump. On his first attempt Owens jumped for a record which held for over 25 years. He hit the mark at 26 feet 8 1/4 inches.

In a few minutes he lined up to run the 220-yard dash. This is a long race at top speed. He set the new world's record at 20.3 seconds. Owens had to do this at full speed.

One more important event was waiting for him. How would he do in the 220-yard low hurdles? Running is one thing, but running and jumping is something else. Owens tore across the track leaping over each stand. His new record was 22.6 seconds.

When Jesse finished his amazing day, the sickness which chased him caught up. He collapsed and had to be helped from the field.

There are many great days in sports: The day the four-minute mile was first run; the day Hank Aaron broke Ruth's home run record.

There is a "great" day coming, however, which will be different from any other day. Jesus Christ has promised to return.

Jesse Owens broke one world's record and tied another while he was still in high school in Cleveland, Ohio.

"I am sure that God who began a good work within you will keep right on helping you grow in his grace until his task within you is finally finished on that day when Jesus Christ returns" (Phil. 1:6, TLB).

We don't know what that day will be like. We do know for sure it will be a day to celebrate.

1. What school did Jesse Owens attend?
2. Name the four events in which Owens set a record on that "great" day.

Let each good day remind us that there will be a great day coming.

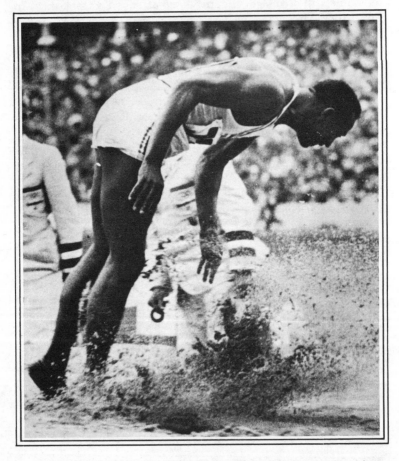

Jesse Owens sets a new world broad-jump record at the Olympics.

twenty-one

She Won by Losing

When Diana Nyad was 16 she was finished as a swimmer. She had trained hard to make the Olympic team but this setback was too much. Diana had an infection in her heart valve and swimming was just too difficult.

She enjoyed the sport too much to quit. Keeping herself in good shape, she reached out for new feats to conquer. Later Diana swam around Manhattan Island in less than eight hours. Miss Nyad then became the first person to swim across Lake Ontario.

It wasn't always a list of victories. Three times she tried to cross the famous English Channel. Three times she had to give up.

Twelve years had passed since she gave up her dream for the Olympics. Now—at 28—Diana decided to try for the biggest challenge of them all. She hoped to become the first person to swim from Cuba to Key West, Florida. If she could do it, the trip would take 60 hours of swimming. The total distance: 110 miles.

The length of the swim would stop most of us. In this case there were several parts which made it even more dangerous. For one thing the waters in that area are filled with sharks with razor sharp teeth. Other swimmers who have tried have had to leave the water because of the man killers.

Not only were the sea animals dangerous, but the choppy waters were hazardous. The waves could hit high and hard.

Diana was determined. She began to plan and organize. A crew of helpers had to be collected. Money had to be raised to make it possible.

Finally $150,000 was raised. The specially built shark cage alone cost $45,000.

Miss Nyad understood the difficulty of her swim and didn't take it lightly. Her daily training was tiring. She lifted weights and ran 12 miles a day. Then Diana would spend seven hours swimming. Her heart was strong and she would be ready.

When the day came to start, the large shark cage was ready at Ortegosa Beach near Havana, Cuba. Diana's body was greased and she entered the water. If everything went well, the trip would take two and a half days of swimming.

Not far out the water itself became a problem. Diana expected waves one foot high to hit her. Instead, the waves were six feet and slowed her greatly.

During the first day Miss Nyad was strong and swam well despite the rough sea. Then she started to tire and had to rest in the water. She could float on her back until she felt ready to start again.

Diana was fed soup, crackers, peanut butter and yogurt through a tube reaching her mouth. She had to eat often to keep up her strength.

As she tired she began to see imaginary things. She thought there were spiders moving in the water.

Miss Nyad's problems kept growing larger. A jellyfish stung her. The jellyfish in the tropics can be terribly painful. Salt water was making her lips crack. Her tongue began to puff to a huge size.

Diana had been swimming for 42 hours. If she was on course the trip would take another 18. Then the most crushing news of all came. They had gone off course and were not heading for Florida. It would take another 50 hours to reach Key West. She had to give up.

Whatever Diana tries the rest of her athletic career, she is already a winner. It is a long way from a faulty heart valve at 16 to trying to swim the open seas. She got there by a tough determination and tremendously hard work.

Life is filled with stop signs. Many people get discouraged and quit. They are told they are too short, too tall, too weak or too sick. But it is amazing how many people overcome these setbacks and become winners. They hang in there when it's terribly tough.

Sometimes it is just as tough to follow Jesus Christ. He said it would be. We get tired of trying to stay clean. Once in a while our friends laugh at us. It would be easy to throw up our hands and say "I can't."

"Cling tightly to your faith in Christ and always keep your conscience clear, doing what you know is right" (1 Tim. 1:19, TLB).

You may lose sometimes, just as Diana Nyad did. But you are a much better person because you are willing to try.

1. Name two places Diana swam successfully.
2. Can you name another athlete who overcame an early set-back?

We can't win every time, but we can give it all we have.

twenty-two

The Biggest Thief

When Lou Brock became a major league base-
ball player, stealing bases didn't mean much. Hitting home runs
was what counted.

But Brock began to steal a few here and a couple there. Soon
he was starting to enjoy it and the total began to add up.

In 1974 the St. Louis outfielder had learned to steal so well he
set a new record. During that season he stole 118 bases.

What kind of lightning speed does this man have? Is he the
fastest runner to ever play baseball? Probably not. The secret to
his success has been the ability to study pitchers.

Brock watches for a certain position in the pitcher's stand or
the way he holds his arm. When the pitcher looks like he will
throw slowly, Lou takes off for second.

Because he has made a science out of stealing, Brock has done
what faster men could not. In 164 games he stole 118 bases. He
became one of the most exciting players in the game.

One big year wasn't enough for Lou. After playing for fifteen
seasons, Brock had a chance to break the big record.

Ty Cobb had stolen the most bases of any player. When the
"Georgia Peach" retired 50 years before, he had stolen a total of
893 bases. For half a century no one could equal this number.

Brock at 38 was closing in on the mark. If he could catch it, he
would do it faster than Cobb had. Cobb played for the Detroit
Tigers a huge 24 seasons. Brock was trying to break the record
after only 16 years.

The tension was high as Lou got closer to the magic number.

Some days he seemed nervous. Other days he couldn't steal a base no matter how hard he tried.

Finally the big day came. The St. Louis Cardinals were playing the San Diego Padres. In the first inning Brock walked. As he waited on first base, Lou had made up his mind. On the first pitch he took off flying for second. When he slid into the bag his whole team came running out to shake his hand. Lou Brock had tied Ty Cobb.

In the seventh inning Brock stole another base. He was now the biggest thief in baseball.

Some people are fast but foolish. Their legs can really move but they don't think before they run.

We see some running after they have stolen something. Others are running to hide from work. Still others have run from the police for years and they are afraid to stop.

Speed doesn't mean much if the runner doesn't use his head. If he is smart he will learn to run first of all toward God. After he knows Him, the runner is better prepared to face life. If he forgets about God, he may run all his life and end the race sad and disappointed.

"The Lord is a strong fortress. The godly run to him and are safe" (Prov. 18:10, TLB).

To run away from God is life's most foolish mistake. To run toward God is to find the purpose of living.

1. Have you ever gotten into trouble for running? How?
2. How can a person begin running toward God?

It makes more sense to run wisely than to run fast.

twenty-three

Foyt's Greatest Race

Every year Indianapolis becomes the most famous city in America for auto racing. Fans come from all over the country to watch the colorful 500-mile contest. With speeds close to 200 miles per hour some amazing tests of cars and men are seen.

One of the most exciting races in recent years involved A. J. Foyt. An excellent driver each year, 1977 proved his big day at Indy.

Three times before, Foyt had won the big event. But by now it had been a long time. Ten years had passed since the skillful driver had wheeled into Victory Lane at Indy. Now in his forties, spectators wondered if he could do it again.

This year was going to be different no matter who won. For the first time a woman was going to be driving in the race. Not just anyone can enter. First there are different tryouts. Both the car and the driver have to prove they can race. A lot of people go home disappointed.

Janet Guthrie wrote her name into the history books by becoming that "first woman." She only completed 27 laps during the Indy race, but she opened a new place for ladies.

Guthrie got the publicity, but Foyt kept his eye on the race. This contest had been held for 61 years and no one had ever won it four times. Foyt had a chance, but maybe he was too old.

The race in 1977 had gone only fifty miles before the front runners were in position. Gordon Johncock was in first place and A. J. Foyt was breathing on his neck in second.

Johncock was an excellent driver and could easily win the race. In a test run he became the only person to go 200 miles an hour at the Indy track.

Foyt couldn't gain the lead and Johncock was holding a steady pace. They had raced 460 miles, 184 laps around the track. Unless Foyt could soon make his move, the day was lost.

Only 15 laps to go. Speeds had reached 196 miles an hour. Foyt was 6.8 seconds behind Johncock. Then suddenly a cloud of blue smoke puffed into the air. It came from Johncock's engine. His motor had blown out and his race was over. Slowly his car coasted to the side and Foyt roared on.

Will Foyt be happy with four wins? Or will he go for a magic number five? He merely says, "Why not? Maybe the good Lord will want A. J. to win next year, too."

It would have been easy for Foyt to stay out of the race. After all, he had won before. Ten years had passed since he had last won. Why keep on trying?

But Foyt had fight. Somebody was going to win and he decided it might as well be he.

It is easy to get sloppy and not care. Some young people slough off in school because they don't care. Others do their jobs halfway because they are lazy. They don't care if they win or not and they probably never will.

James was concerned about this attitude. Lots of things in life are tough, but that's no reason to give up on them.

"Blessed is the man who perseveres under trial, because when he has stood the test, he will receive the victor's crown, the life God has promised to those who love him" (James 1:12, NIV).

Everyone who gives life his best wins. They may not come in first place, but they win just because they tried.

1. Name two things you would like to do but are afraid to try.
2. Can you name some time when God might get discouraged?

Help me do a good job in everything I do.

A. J. Foyt after winning his fourth Indianapolis 500 race in 1977.

twenty-four

Just a "Kid"

Young people do amazing things. Matt Hodges of St. Albans, West Virginia, won a Karate black belt when he was only six years old. He is the youngest person to ever win one.

Sports have never been reserved just for adults. Some of the most amazing accomplishments have been achieved by teenagers and younger children. Sonja Henie won the world's figure skating championship when she was 13. Karen Muir set a world swimming record at 12. Bob Mathias won the Olympic decathlon at 17.

One of the finest young athletes has been a "kid" named Chris Evert. Chris has developed into one of the best female tennis players of our time. No one could tell her to "come back when you grow up." She started competing with and beating adults while she was still a young lady.

Chris came from a tennis family. This didn't make her a championship player, but the influence helped. Her dad was a tennis instructor in Fort Lauderdale, Florida. They lived just half a mile from the courts and got there often.

At the age of six Chris began her tennis career. It wasn't an exciting start. Her father would take her to the tennis courts and throw balls to her. It isn't easy when you are a first grader, so Chris missed more than she hit. But she got better. Her father offered Chris little prizes if she could hit ten balls. They stuck with it and she caught on.

Chris Evert is a good "natural" athlete, but tennis didn't come easily. At the age of seven she was practicing four hours every day. On the weekends it rose to nine hours.

The hard work was beginning to pay off. At eight years of age she won her first trophy. She played often and won more. When Chris was 11 she had a national ranking.

Other young people had made it in tennis early so she was encouraged. In some sports teenagers are not allowed to compete with adults. Tennis was different and Chris aimed directly for the top. "Mo" Connolly had won the Wightman Cup at only 16 and the Wimbledon at the ages of 17, 18 and 19. All young people had to do was prove themselves.

Chris had fantastic skills but she also had weaknesses. Players caught on to her back-hand stroke. When she had to move to her left, Chris had trouble bringing a sharply hit ball back. If she was to play against the adults, some help had to be found.

Since her dad was an instructor he suggested a solution. When a ball was hit far to her left Chris was told to grab the racket with both hands. It looked strange for a player of her ability to hold a racket that way. It did the job. The audience could laugh if they wanted but she would win anyway.

Her sports career was progressing excellently. At 15 she was ready to play some of the best tennis players in the world. She defeated a French professional that year. Later Chris beat the Wimbledon champion. She had made it almost to the top and she was still a middle teenager.

Finally Chris met the biggest name in women's tennis: Billy Jean King. Chris was 16 now and at the top. The crowd went wild as the two magnificent athletes battled back and forth. Her famous two-handed back hand came in handy as the struggle moved. The final winner: Chris Evert, a teenager from Fort Lauderdale.

Naturally she couldn't accept the prize money. Chris was still an amateur.

Young people are often smart and have good ability. They take responsibility and show how grown up they can be. Others slough off and get into trouble. It all depends on what we want to do.

"Don't let anyone think little of you because you are young" (1 Tim. 4:12, TLB).

What adults think of young people often depends on the be-
havior of the person. Today's youth are intelligent and capable.
Many are proving that God has given them much ability.

1. How old was Chris Evert when she won her first trophy?
2. Do adults trust young people? Should they?

We can be an example in our youth.

twenty-five

Musial's Big Day

They called him Stan the Man in St. Louis where he played baseball for 22 years. During that time Musial set 60 records, including 3,036 hits.

Like Babe Ruth, Stan started out as a pitcher, but he was too good a hitter to stay there. This smart move allowed him to win the Most Valuable Player award three times in the National League.

Naturally, Musial had many big days in his baseball career. But none was more spectacular than September 22, 1946, in Boston.

Stan had three games during that season in which he collected five safe hits. Only the great Ty Cobb had ever done it four times in one season.

This wasn't a good day to try for the record. To begin with, Warren Spahn was pitching, and presently he was the best in the league. If this wasn't hard enough, a second factor made it close to impossible.

During the three days before, the St. Louis Cardinals had played Brooklyn. In one game Stan had injured his left wrist and it hurt to swing. Some players would have sat out the game, but Musial loved to play. He decided to swallow hard and give it the best courage he had.

Since he didn't have much strength that day, Stan knew what he had to do. He would have to swing on the first pitch. His wrists couldn't take twenty hard twists.

The first time at bat Spahn sent a sizzling pitch and Musial looped it into left field for a single. The second time up he smashed a powerful double over the left fielder's head. So far two pitches and two hits.

Spahn got himself into trouble and was out of the game when Musial came to the plate the third time. The new pitcher unwound and Stan couldn't wait. People rose to their feet as the ball went sailing into the bullpen for a home run.

By the time he came to bat the fourth time it all looked easy. Stan sent a quick chop over the shortstop's head for a single.

The fifth visit to the batter's box had everyone excited. Boston brought in a rookie pitcher. Musial was one hit away from tying Cobb. If the new pitcher got wild and walked Stan, the record would be gone.

Here came the windup. The pitcher threw his foot forward and unleashed the ball. Musial smashed it into the ground and took off for first. The ball went tearing through the infield past the fielders. Stan was on first and had his fifth hit.

It was a hard day, but Musial did what he knew he had to do. He didn't watch one ball go by or foul one off. The Man got five hits on exactly five pitched balls.

"So take a new grip with your tired hands, stand firm on your shaky legs, and mark out a straight smooth path for your feet so that those who follow you, though weak and lame, will not fall and hurt themselves, but become strong" (Heb. 12:12, 13, TLB).

Sometimes it takes an extra amount of strength and courage to follow Jesus Christ. Even when we are tired and would like to give up, we need to stick to it. Christ understands and tells us to hang in there. You can do it. It would be easy to live against God. But after we give it that extra fight, we will be glad we decided to listen to Christ.

1. When is it hardest for you to obey God?
2. Have you ever thought, "Baloney, I wish I weren't a Christian"? Explain.

It's tough to always do what is right. God needs to help me stick it out.

Stan Musial has a lifetime batting average of .340.

twenty-six

The Golden Jet

Would you like to become a star hockey player? Here is one way to start. Get a pair of skates when you are four years old. Live in Canada where it is cold for many months. Have a father who loves to skate every day. Now, there are other ways to become a hockey star, but this is how Bobby Hull did it.

Hockey is a tough sport. It is fast and rough. It is hard to be a superstar in hockey. Yet, some have played well into middle age. The all-time high scorer in hockey is Gordie Howe. He still played at the age of 50. His two sons played on the same team with him. Bobby Hull is one of these strong superstars.

Many of the best stars come from Canada. Children are organized into little leagues just like baseball and football in the United States. There are a few leagues in the States but not nearly as many as in Canada.

Bobby Hull grew up in these leagues. Even in grade school it was obvious he was an outstanding player. By the age of 12 he was playing on adult teams. At this early age many old-timers knew Bobby would someday be a professional hockey player.

The Chicago Black Hawks soon became interested in Bobby. At 14 they signed him to a contract and he started to play on some of their minor teams. When he was 18 he had made it to the club. Bobby became one of the youngest players ever to join a professional hockey team.

During his first two years he played regularly and learned his way around. The pros could be mean and he often found himself crashing to the ice. He was determined to fight back like anyone else.

In his third year with the Black Hawks he let everyone know he was a superstar. Bobby scored 39 goals and 42 assists to lead

Bobby Hull in action for the Chicago Black Hawks

the league. He was clocked skating 28 miles an hour. This made him the fastest skater in the league. Fans soon called him the Golden Jet because of his flashy blond hair and rocket speed.

If there was ever a "natural" hockey player it was Hull. He could smash a puck over 100 miles an hour. More than once his speeding puck would knock a goalie or other player down.

Sometimes the game became tough on Hull. Once while playing the Detroit Red Wings a player smashed a hockey stick across Bobby's face. His nose was broken. Hull came back a few days later and had it rebroken. Still he played as soon as he could. There was no place he would rather be than on the ice.

Hockey has never been known for its easiness. After 30 years of playing Gordie Howe had collected 500 stitches in his face alone. Hull hadn't played that long, but he still could count over 200.

On March 12, 1966, Hull wrote his name into the record book again. No player had ever scored more than 50 goals in one season. On that day he smashed a score against the New York Rangers and became the first player with 51.

The fans stopped the game. They stood shouting and screaming. They had seen an athlete do something no one else had done before. And he had done it in the terribly rough sport of hockey.

Some athletes are really great. If you and I had played hockey since we were four, we still would not have been superstars. A great athlete is a rare thing.

But before we throw the word "great" around too much, we should stop and think. There is one who is greater than all of us. Hockey, baseball, football and every other sport will pass away. The only lasting greatness is God himself.

"For the Lord is great beyond description, and greatly to be praised" (Ps. 96:4, TLB).

If we become fantastic athletes and fail to worship God, we have missed real greatness. More than awards, cheering crowds and huge salaries; more than quick hands, sharp sight and fast feet is to know God. Life does not become complete until we have met God in Jesus Christ. God will always be the greatest.

1. How old was Bobby Hull when he joined the Black Hawks?
2. How many stitches did Howe and Hull need in their faces?

Greatness is empty without God.

twenty-seven

The Double Winner

Many young boys have dreamed of becoming a famous running back—to grab that brown ball and tear through the line with crowds screaming. For Archie Griffin it became far more than a dream.

Before his college career was over he became the best running back in football.

As many great stars before him, Griffin decided to attend Ohio State University. He had grown up in Ohio but didn't have to play there. With his high school record Archie could have gone almost anywhere. Over 150 colleges were in touch with him.

But college is much harder than high school. Many athletes can't even make the team.

His first year at Ohio State, he let college football know he was something different. The record for an O.S.U. player was 229 yards in one game. Exceeding that record was probably the farthest thing from Griffin's mind when Woody Hayes put him in the game. The record had stood for over 25 years.

Griffin barreled into the game. Each time they handed him the ball he slashed, spun and dodged forward for yards. When the afternoon was over Archie had run 239 to set a new school record. Griffin was only 18 years old. The Ohio State fans went wild.

This was just the beginning for Griffin, however. During his four years at college he ran a total of 5,177 yards. He carried the ball for more than 100 yards in 31 games in a row. Each game he averaged 123.4 yards. Each time he took the ball he averaged 5.5 yards.

Ohio State's stadium holds almost 90,000 fans. During the

103

four years that Griffin played, the stadium was usually packed out. Fans came to see a star running back. Instead, they were watching a young man totally dependent upon someone else's strength. Before each game Griffin got alone to read his Bible and pray. He knew there was more to life than an athletic program. He also knew that his skill was not enough. He needed Jesus' help. So Archie told his friends what Jesus Christ meant to him.

Griffin was barely large enough to play football. He was only 5 feet 8 inches tall. His playing weight was a small 180 pounds. It is a wonder some of the huge linemen didn't break his bones. But they didn't. Archie didn't miss one game during his entire college program.

At the end of each season college teams hope to go to bowl games. The game with the largest crowd and the most money for the school is the Rose Bowl. Any year Ohio State wins its conference championship they get to go to this important bowl game.

During Griffin's four years at O.S.U. they went to the Rose Bowl every year.

With this kind of record many honors came Griffin's way. Twice he was named Athlete of the Year. But there was one award which was even more special.

Every year the Heisman Trophy is awarded to the best college football player. Stars like Tony Dorsett, Earl Campbell, O. J. Simpson and Billy Sims have won this honor.

Archie Griffin was so good he won the Heisman Trophy during his junior year. A few others had won it as juniors—four to be exact, including Roger Staubach. But no one had yet won it twice.

Would the trophy help his senior year? Would it put so much pressure on him he would go down? His last year at O.S.U. was outstanding. In December, 1975, the word came: Archie Griffin became the first player to win the Heisman Trophy twice.

Few men ever deserved it more. Griffin was a winner both on and off the field.

It is usually hard to handle honors like this. Many athletes, students, and artists let honors change them. They become proud, stuck-up, hard to get along with. They act like spoiled children. Those who knew him said it didn't happen to Archie Griffin.

"Don't praise yourself; let others do it" (Prov. 27:2, TLB).

Cincinnati Bengals running back Archie Griffin grinds for extra yardage while Pittsburgh linebackers try to bring him down.

Have you ever listened to someone who is always telling you how great they are? They brag on and on. They forget to praise God because they are too busy praising themselves.

1. What O.S.U. record did Griffin set?
2. Who else won the Heisman Trophy while a junior?

Give us confidence without becoming self-centered.

twenty-eight

Strike Out Ty Cobb?

Ty Cobb may have been the best baseball player who ever carried a glove. He didn't hit as many home runs as Babe Ruth or Hank Aaron, but he was a great batter.

For three seasons he batted over 400 and had the highest average in the league for years. They called him the "Georgia Peach" because he was born in the South. He stole more bases than anyone else. It took years for anyone to break his records.

Cobb was the most famous player who ever wore a Detroit Tiger uniform. He played ball back in the days when baseball players were often rough and mean. He could be as tough as the worst of them. Pity the poor second baseman when Cobb stole a base. He slid hard, fast and kept his spikes high to scare the fielders. If you got mad at him, he was ready to fight in a second.

When Cobb was a big star there was a young pitcher who played on a team in northern Michigan. His name was Edgar Pace and he was a good ball player. Each game he was paid $10 for pitching, and he hoped some day to get on a major league team.

Pace's name was getting in the paper regularly. Sometimes he struck out 17 batters in one game. He felt the time had come to try the major leagues, so he wrote a letter to the general manager of the Detroit Tigers.

He offered to come to Detroit and pitch to the famous Ty Cobb. If he did, he promised to strike out the Georgia Peach in three throws.

Attendance at the ball park hadn't been very good lately so the general manager thought it over. Why not? Publicize the match in the paper and bring the young star to Detroit.

The day finally came and people packed the stadium. So everyone could watch, the regular game was held off for half an hour. The whole town was buzzing. Could a young pitcher strike out baseball's most famous hitter in just three pitches?

Pace went to the mound and started to warm up. He looked confident as he rubbed the new ball in his hands. Each practice pitch was as straight as a ruler and faster than a train. The ball hit the catcher's mitt with a crisp thump. The audience sounded like a beehive.

Cobb came up to the batter's box and applause broke out from the crowd. He bent his body into its familiar stance. No foolishness. He was ready to send this kid back to the bush leagues.

Pace wasted no time. He leaned back, wound up and sent his first pitch whistling. Cobb swung a sharp bat and sent the ball screaming into center field. The crowd cheered.

Unmoved, Pace threw a second ball and Cobb smashed it against the right field wall. A third pitch and Cobb hit it like a bullet right at the pitcher.

Finally the manager came out to the mound and said, "Well, what do you say?" Pace looked him in the eye, handed him the ball and said, "I don't believe that was Ty Cobb."

"Don't brag about your plans for tomorrow—wait and see what happens" (Prov. 27:1, TLB).

People get tired of braggers. If someone asks us if we can swim and we say yes, it isn't bragging. They asked us a question, and we told the truth. But if we tell people we get better grades than they do, we are bragging.

Whether we are children or adults, we should avoid bragging. If not, our friends may avoid us.

1. What is bragging?
2. When is it all right to say you can do something?

Heavenly Father, teach us to choose our words well. Bragging gets us into trouble and sometimes makes us lie.

Ty Cobb was the greatest baseball player of his time

twenty-nine

Shoot the Rapids

E very year thousands of people get ready for one of America's most exciting sports. They travel to Colorado to ride 277 miles of rough water in wooden boats.

The trip may take 14 days and allows for plenty of camping. Each night the passengers sleep along the river bank. When daylight breaks, they eat a large breakfast and then start down the raging waters.

The water moves so fast the boats often become swamped. The passengers then have to grab a bucket and start bailing.

It is an exciting, memorable journey but the danger is kept at a minimum. The National Park Service refuses to allow anyone on the spraying rapids without life jackets. Years ago some people drowned without proper equipment, so now the rules are strictly kept.

Today a number of professional guides take sportsmen on these trips. Some of their boats are made of wood while others are rubber. The trip may be for the courageous, but more are trying it every year. As many as 14,000 now sign up for the adventure.

It's hard to imagine the speed of the river. At places it reaches 20,000 cubic feet per second. The boat will hit one wave and go up into the air as if it were about to fly. The next minute the craft will sink low in the river with water pouring in.

The season doesn't begin until the middle of June, but that is plenty early. The water is only 55°. When the passengers get soaked they wish they had a heater.

For those who don't want to be alone, the larger boats hold 30 people. Others carry a mere 5.

Between dodging waves and emptying buckets, the adventurer can look up at beautiful mountains. They rise hundreds of feet into the air and are decorated with beautiful colors. Every once in a while the river becomes calm as glass and nature stands quietly around.

At night the wildlife along the river bank will sing everyone to sleep. But no one rests too long. In eight hours they are all back on the bouncing boats again.

Shooting the rapids isn't for people who like to watch. It's one sport where everybody is right in the middle of the action.

Anyone who gets the chance to take this trip can enjoy the beauty of God's creation. He can see the handsomely carved hills which the wind has shaped. He can see the dancing, often raging, river smashing against the rocks.

When night comes, the river adventurer will lie on the ground by the bank. Over his head will float the soft clouds, diamond-like stars and peaceful moon.

In the middle of this beauty he can say God is real and God is good. Nature is sending out a message for us to believe in our great Creator.

"When I look into the night skies and see the work of your fingers—the moon and the stars you have made—I cannot understand how you can bother with mere puny man, to pay any attention to him!" (Ps. 8:3, 4, TLB).

1. Do you think the world could have existed without a creator? Why?
2. Why was our world made? Give your opinion.

Nature doesn't tell us everything about God, but it shows us something.